CACOPHONY

CACOPHONY

TRISTA WOOJIN

.:||X||:.

I

Ode to the Elixir of Life

In twilight's murky embrace, a dark allure,
Emanates from the celestial noir,

From depths unseen, an elegy unfurls,
As shadows dance through reverent whirls.

Oh, coffee divine, thy essence beckons,
A mistress of dusk, thy fragrance reckons,

Like seraphic whispers, enchanting the air,
Drawing pulses yearning for a taste so rare.

In tendrils of smoke, secrets commence,
A symphony of bitterness, sublime in its sense,

Embraced by ebony as moonlight cascades,
A solace discovered in opalescent shades.

Silken tendrils entwined, offering solace,
In intricate patterns, the heartache it erases,

An elixir of ardent verses unsung,
Fleeting moments caught beneath shadows hung.

Oh, how the blackened elixir cascades,
Stirring longing within, as night fades,

From porcelain lips, a sip, an artful dance,
Unveiling enchantment in transient chance.

Ethereal desires penned on parchment stark,
A soliloquy birthed in the depths of the dark.

Linger, bewitch, and kindle my desires,
Oh, coffee divine, stoke my innermost fires

II

Conundrum

Does the vast, empty cosmos dream of us,
Lost in its celestial expanse?
Or are we mere specks,
Forgotten whispers in an eternal dance?
Do we float within its thoughts,
Like galaxies drifting through the night?
Or are we but illusions,
Figments of a lost cosmic light?
Where does a thought go when it's forgotten,
When its essence fades away?
Does it drift through the cosmos,
A whisper lost in the fray?
A prisoner to the depths of oblivion,
Bound by time's cruel hand,
Or do these forgotten thoughts transcend,
Part of a timeless band?

Do we have free will, or is everything predestined,
Entwined in fate's demise?
Are we the marionettes, dancing on strings,

Controlled by unseen ties?
Do choices mold our destiny,
Or are we trapped in an endless loop?
A puppeteer's creation,
A play scripted by a timeless troop?
What is the purpose of setting goals,
If we all succumb to death's call?
Do they give our lives meaning,
Or are they illusions, destined to fall?
Can achievements and aspirations defy the void,
A monument to our existence?
Or with each passing breath,
Do they crumble, lost to transient distance?
Is it possible to know what is truly good
And what is evil's vile domain?
In a realm of moral ambiguity,
Does clarity forever wane?
Do we stumble through the darkness,
Searching for a truth untold?
Or are we mere reflections,
mirrors of a gray soul, trapped within mold?
Why are you here at this very moment,
In the tapestry of your life?
Are you the author of your fate,
Or a pawn in a cosmic strife?
Do chance encounters shape your path,
Or is there purpose to each twist?
A random existence in a cosmic sea,
Or a destiny that cannot resist?
If we need to follow rules at all costs,
Then why do exceptions find their way?
Do these contradictions bind us,
Or do they lead astray?
Are rules but illusions,

Fading echoes of a society's design?
Or are they the foundations,
Morals woven into divine?
Is there an end to the universe,
or does it stretch into infinity's embrace?
Does existence fold upon itself,
Or does eternity carry its grace?
Does time recede into forever,
Or is it but a finite realm?
A vast expanse, or a fragile thread,
Be it stagnant or forever overwhelm?
What is the purpose and meaning of time,
An enigma we cannot deny?
Does it measure existence,
Or is it an illusion we forever defy?
Does it shape our experiences,
Or confine us in a temporal hold?
Is it a gift or a curse,
Forever weaving unraveling stories untold?

Do our human accomplishments hold significance
Beyond the mortal veil?
Will they echo in eternity,
Or wither into nothingness stale?
Do they stand as testaments,
Monuments to our collective might?
Or are they whispers in the wind,
Fleeting dreams lost in cosmic night?
If you're trying to fail and you succeed,
Did you fail or did you succeed?
A conundrum of paradoxes, a riddle we forever misread.
Does success yield failure,
Or does failure bear success in its core?
Two sides of a twisted coin, forever intertwined evermore.

If you expect the unexpected,
Doesn't that make the unexpected expected?
A paradox that defies reason,
Where logic stands unprotected.
Does anticipation hold power,
Or does unpredictability forever sway?
Can chaos be tamed,
Or does surprise forever hold sway?
How is it possible that the world is in debt,
When debt is but an illusion's play?
A construct of man, numbers entwined,
A fragile realm astray.
Does wealth hold power,
Or is it a mere facade, a game of make-believe?
A matrix of numbers and greed,
Where deception is the thieves' reprieve.
What would a room made of mirrors look like,
Devoid of reflections therein?
A void of infinite reflections,
A paradox hidden within.
Would it be a void, empty and cold,
Or a labyrinth of endless echoes?
A room of self-reflection, a prison or solace,
Where truth forever flows?

III

Lady Nox Aeterna

Night fell upon the weary world, an inevitable descent,
Cloaking all in its embrace, a shroud of shadows, silently sent.
The darkness seeped through every crevice, every crack and seam,
And as it spread, it whispered secrets, haunting like a midnight dream.
The night was a mistress, her ebony veil so thin,
Like a sleazy dress, worn and worn, concealing forbidden sin.
She seduced, leaving the hearts of men entangled in her spell,
A temptress of the clandestine, conjurer of a haunting, torturous knell.
Beneath this darkened tapestry, the secrets of the world dwell,
Unveiling truths that daylight hides,
casting shadows that foretell. Within her depths, all fears awaken,
Like phantoms lost and forlorn,
In this velvety abyss, where the darkest secrets are cruelly born.
Within the night's bosom, secrets dance and linger,
Silent whispers unheard, every hint of darkness they bring her.
She holds the stories of broken hearts, of love's bitter betrayal,
Concealing the pain of weary souls, lost in a desolate, endless trail.
In the depths of shadows, eyes reflect a silent yearning,

Obsidian pools of forgotten dreams, where darkness is discerning.
And as night unfolds, it envelopes each soul with a chilling embrace,
An ever-present reminder of life's transient, ephemeral space.
No starlight dare pierce this shroud, no moon dares to shine,
For the night delights in her dominion, presiding over the divine.
Her ebony hands stretch, touching the wounds of a world always aching,
As she weaves her presence through the tapestry of secrets she's taking.
Yet with her alluring presence, she ignites the spark of desire,
An intoxicating blend of pleasure and pain, that sets everything on fire.
Within her arms, the veils of morality fade and crumble away,
And in this sea of darkness, human nature's flaws are on full display.
Night fell, the darkness thin, like some sleazy dress that's been worn

IV

Confession

In this realm of existence, I must confess,
There's a habit people call a source of zest,
But try as I might, I can't embrace its charm,
For daily walks only bring me harm.
They swear by their strides, their feet on the ground,
Claiming joy and health in leaps they have found.
But to me, the pavement holds no allure,
As I trod along, and my spirit grows unsure.
The sun may shine and the breeze may blow,
Yet with each step, my energy seems to go.
The birds sing their songs with melodious glee,
But my mind wanders to other places, you see.
The world, they say, is mine to explore,
But the confines of this path leave me wanting more.
For joy should not be found in measured steps,
But in the wild chaos where my heart leaps and reps.
Meditation, ah yes, the mystical art,
Whispered secrets to calm the raging heart.
Oh, the serenity it's said to bring,
But in silence, my mind begins to sing.

The quietude unveiled, a tempest within,
Thoughts swirling, colliding, a cacophony of din.
How can I find peace when chaos reigns supreme?
In the whirlwinds of my thoughts, I seek my dream.

Pedicures, oh what a luxury they proclaim,
To pamper the toes, to soothe away the pain.
But I find no solace in the touch of the brush,
As my feet long for the earth, for the mud, for the rush.
For beneath the layers of polish and shine,
Restless soles yearn for freedom divine.
To wander barefoot, connected to the ground,
To feel the earth's heartbeat, the very same sound.
Family meetings, a gathering so grand,
Where bonds are strengthened with every command.
But forced interactions, stifled expressions,
Leave me questioning genuine connections.
Contrived smiles and inauthentic laughter,
Is this the true essence of what we're after?
I seek solace in solitude's embrace,
Where my spirit can dance, finding its own space.
Naps, the epitome of relaxation's delight,
A coveted respite in the midst of life's fight.
But as my head hits the pillow's soft embrace,
Dreams elude me, forever lost in the chase.
Restless imagination, a mind that never sleeps,
In my wakefulness, my soul finds respite deep.
In the quiet moments when the world slumbers on,
I find solace in darkness, where dreams are born.
Camping, they proclaim, a nature-filled divine,
To seek serenity beneath the starlit sky.
But as the tent closes in, and the firelight fades,
My heart yearns for the comfort of my own home's shades.
The lure of adventure, the outdoors so vast,

Yet my sanctuary lies not in nature, but in the past.
In aging pages, stories and tales,
Where my imagination soars, and my spirit prevails.
Kale, oh green leafy wonder of health,
A superfood to nourish one's innermost self.
But as I chew on its bitterness, my taste buds cry,
For the sweetness of indulgence that makes them fly.
For my joy resides not in rigid restraint,
But in culinary exploration, no rules to taint.
In flavors and spices, where pleasure is found,
In the symphony of tastes that leave me spellbound.
So let them walk, meditate, and gather near,
Let them nap, camp, and consume what's sheer.
As I dance through the realms of my vibrant mind,
Creating worlds anew, where no boundaries bind.

V

Blood in the Street

The first thing I saw was a puddle of blood in the street,
An omen of terror, a tale yet to complete,
In the town of sorrow, where the moon seldom peeks,
Lay a secret so profound, the past plagued its streets
Haunted whispers echoed under a forever gloomy sky,
Where nightmares were birthed, where hope came to die.
Once adorned with laughter, now consumed by despair,
A sinister presence cast an eternal pallor in the air,
In its horrid depth grew whispers of a forsaken blade,
A malevolence so wicked, a relentless cascade.
I wandered through ashen streets with trepidation and dread,
Eyes meeting eyes, all pleading, yet none filled with thread,
Ghastly faces, empty husks, devoid of all life,
Victims silenced by the darkness, slaughtered with a knife
The first thing I saw was a puddle of blood in the street

The Last Whisper

I am so tired, I want to sleep for a week,
But the haunting whispers refuse to leave,
They coil around me, suffocating my mind,
In the endless darkness, solace I cannot find.
In the pale embrace of the night's cold kiss,
I find no solace, only the abyss,
The weight of the world, too heavy to bear,
I long for respite, for a moment to spare.
Beneath the mourning veil of the starless sky,
I whisper my secrets, my silent cry,
But the darkness swallows my words whole,
I am so tired, I want to sleep for a week,
To escape the torment, the sorrow that reeks,
But even in slumber, the nightmares will keep,
And I'll wander in darkness, lost in the deep.
As the veil of dawn gently brushes the sky,
So I'll linger a while in the shadow's embrace
I am so tired, I want to sleep for a week

VII

Ascent

Within the turbulent tempest of the mind,
Lies a landscape of chaos, undefined,
Where thunderous thoughts clash without reprieve,
And raging emotions churn, refusing to leave.
At the onset, a whisper of unease,
A gathering of clouds, a subtle tease,
As the first rumblings of thunder arise,
The tempest within begins its somber rise.
Anger brews, a tempest of rage,
As lightning strikes the mind's dark stage,
The thunderclaps echo the turmoil within,
A symphony of chaos, a deafening din.
The rain falls heavy, a deluge of tears,
Washing away the pain of unspoken fears,
Each droplet a testament to the soul's release,
A cleansing downpour, a moment of peace.

In the heart of the maelstrom, a fleeting calm,
A respite from the mind's relentless qualm,
But the tempest rages, refusing to cease,

As the tumultuous cycle seeks its release.
Slowly, the fury begins to wane,
The tumultuous thoughts, no longer inane,
The thunder fades into a distant lull,
As the storm within surrenders to the soul
In the wake of the tempest's fervent flight,
A tranquil expanse emerges, cloaked in night,
The stars twinkle softly, a beacon of hope,
Guiding the mind through the labyrinth of mope.
At last, the mind finds its tranquil shore,
A haven from the storm's relentless uproar,
Where the echoes of chaos gently subside,
And the tempest within finds solace, purified.

VIII

Petrichoir

I inhale the perfume of ruin and rebirth,
A bitter-sweet mixture, a curse upon this earth
. For in this broken world, I am bound,
A sovereign of shadows, forever crowned.
Though the sky has fallen, its fragments persist,
Buried deep within me, clenched within my fist.
For I am burdened, chained to this desolate place,
The weight of this ownership seeps into my veins,
A constant reminder of my eternal chains.

IX

Cosmic Lament

In the vast expanse of cosmic night,
Where stars ignite and worlds take flight,
Silent void, a canvas black,
Whispers secrets, no turning back.
Planets dance in timeless waltz,
Amidst the void, their presence false.
Nebulas swirl, a cosmic ballet,
Infinite beauty, light years away.
Yet in this grandeur, darkness seeps,
A void so deep, where sorrow keeps.
In the embrace of endless night,

Lonely souls yearn for guiding light.
A celestial elegy, a mournful song,
In the cosmic expanse, they don't belong.
Staggered in space, adrift, forlorn,
In the cosmic dance, their hearts are torn.
For in the grandeur of the astral sea,
They find no solace, no place to be free.
So they wander, lost in cosmic gloom,

In the endless expanse, their spirits consumed.

X

Gormandize

A sinister invitation did infest,
A group of strangers, unaware, their fate, to jest.
Whispers carried on a moonlit breeze,
Summoning souls to an ornate feast,
A wealthy socialite's mansion, grand and rare,
Lured them all through the depths of nightmare.
They arrived at twilight, the moon ablaze,
Under a sky adorned with a macabre haze,
A mansion of opulence, timeless and vast,
Undulating, they fretted, their hearts beating fast.
Heavy doors creaked, revealing the abyss,
A foyer cloaked in eerie gloom, remiss,
Gasping, they reluctantly ventured within,
Unknowing, their essence would soon begin to thin.
The air reeked of dread, a palpable mirth,
Setting their nerves ablaze, an ominous birth,
A banquet room adorned in crimson stains,
Whispering secrets, hiding anguish and pains.
A table, elongated and draped in black,
Awaited each stranger, their destiny sealed, intact,

Seats, once empty, filling with a sense of despair,
They had become the pawns in a cruel billionaire's snare.
Candles flickered in a morose ballet,
Casting haunting glimmers in the dim, eerie display
, The feast awaited, the main course to be revealed,
But no delectable dishes, only flesh would be concealed.
A golden chandelier overhead swayed,
Mingling with their escalating terror, undisplayed,
The socialite, veiled in malevolence, grinned,
Amused by the terror, the darkness within.
Bound by the dread, they perched upon their chairs
, Each stranger's heartbeat throbbed, masked by their stares,
An illusion of camaraderie, shattered and cracked,
Fear etched into their souls, forever tracked.
The socialite raised a glass, eyes gleaming so cold,
Delighting in the torment, the decay to unfold
"My dear guests," she purred, her voice sharp as a blade,
"Gathered here tonight, your essence shall fade."
In horror, they trembled, an unbridled fear,
As she unveiled her true masquerade, so queer,
Eyes alight with crimson, teeth sharpened as knives
, She was no mere hostess; she hungered for their lives.
Dismay filled their eyes with a terror profound,
As servants advanced, silent, shuffling with no sound,
Carrying platters, shrouded in mystic shroud,
Unveiling the grotesque feast, to their horror loud.
Strangers' hearts pounding, breaths strangled, suppressed,
Gagging on the stench, the banquet of distress,
Limbs of strangers, hacked and severed with precision,
Laid bare, presented with a sinister decision.

Each stranger's fate sealed, etched in frightful despair,
To become the main course, a horrid affair,
But in their panic, a glimmer of hope did ignite,

With strength, they charged; it was time to fight.
The socialite's grin contorted with glee,
Amused by their futile rebellion, they would never be fre
e, But the strangers fought mercilessly, possessed by might,
Gored and bloodied, they refused to surrender to the night.

Armed with desperation, they clawed and they bit,
Bodies collided, smearing the halls with crimson spit,
Yet, against them, the socialite stood unbent,
Unyielding in her sadistic intent.

The battle reached its crescendo, screams pierced the air,
But one by one, the strangers sank into despair,
Overwhelmed by the socialite's demonic force,
They succumbed to her hunger, remorseless, no remorse.
Silence fell upon the mansion's desolate halls,
A chorus of conquest echoing through decaying walls,
The socialite, satiated, basked in her gruesome glee,
She had savored their essence, their spirits now set free.

And so, their haunted whispers remain in the land,
A cautionary tale carried by an eerie hand,
Of strangers lured to a cursed abode, their doom,
Bound to remain forever, their souls entombed.

XI

Ephemera

In the shadows of the entryway, where veils of darkness dance,
Lies a tapestry of forgotten treasures, a peculiar second chance.
Cast your gaze upon this realm, where secrets often hide,
And let the words unravel, as darkness intertwines beside.

Softly gleaming by candle-light, a coffee cup holds its place,
A vessel stained with memories, fragments of forgotten grace.
Each sip, a bitter elixir, a taste of life's bitter-sweet,
Mornings steeped in solitude, a journey incomplete.
A blanket sprawls upon the floor, a refuge for weary souls,
Ornaments of warmth and solace, as darkness silently unfolds
Bound within its woven threads, tales of dreams untold,
Where fantasies are whispered, and truths begin to mold.
An ashtray rests with tempered breath, an altar to demise,
Where tendrils of wispy smoke ascend, vanishing to the skies.
Within its shallow depths, lies the remnants of desire, A
testament to worldly cravings, consumed by the fire.
Beside the parchment's scattered ink, a pen discarded, worn,
Its weary nib, now futile, no longer adorned.
Yet once, it danced upon the page, a conduit for the mind,

Echoes of words etched in darkness, now left far behind.
This crossroads oft forgotten, where layers of life entwine,
A threshold 'twixt the realms, where truth and fiction combine.
Bridging the gap, traversing the abyss, where contradictions merge,
Boundaries blurred and shifted, as destinies converge.

For in this twilight haven, where reality meets the dream,
A canvas of existence, suspended in spectral gleam.
The threshold of the mortal world, enigmatic and profound,
Where wonder intertwines with fear, and silence echoes sound

Cradle For The Dead

Upon the murky waters, the rowboat sways,
Tethered to the pier in a haunting ballet.
As dusk descends with an ominous guise,
The boat bobs in rhythm, under darkening skies.
Whispers rise from the depths, a siren's call,
Beckoning the lost, the forsaken, and all.
The water ripples with an eerie refrain,
A harbinger of sorrow, a prelude to pain.
The pier stands silent, a witness to dread,
As the boat rocks gently, like a cradle for the dead.

Shadows dance upon the water's crest,
A macabre waltz, a dirge for the distressed.
In the fading light, the boat's form distorts,
Taking on a semblance of ghostly cohorts.
As night falls, the waters conceal their guise,
Leaving the rowboat to bob under pitch-black skies.
A vessel abandoned, with tales to unfold,
Of lost souls adrift, of mysteries untold.
In the stillness of night, where fear takes hold,

The small rowboat lingers, a story untold.

XIII

Echoes in the Mist

Hope's sweet embers lie forever dead.
Dusk reigns perpetual, the sun, unseen,
And moonlight, but a distant memory.
No vibrant hues adorn this somber scene,
Just shades of gray, devoid of vibrancy.
Twisted trees stand tall, their branches bare,
Like skeletal fingers, reaching for the sky.
No songbirds sing, their melodies so rare,
Silenced by despair's relentless cry.
Here, laughter turns to echoes in the mist,
And joy's warm touch is barren, cold, and bleak.
Love's gentle flame succumbs to ceaseless twist,
A fragile heart now weary and weak.
Where once were cities teeming with delight,
Now naught but ruins, shrouded in despair.

The streets are blanketed in endless night,
As if the world were caught in deathly snare.
Within the souls of men, a darkness dwells,
Concealed beneath their hardened, vacant gaze.

A heavy burden that each heart compels,
And grips their spirits, lost in twisted ways.
No glimmer shines through windows darkened, sealed,
Inhabitants consumed by melancholy's sting.

A fate devoid of light, forever sealed,
In this alternate reality's cruel wing.
Yet still, a single hope refuses to resign,
A flicker in the depths of ruins grand.
A spark that whispers of a world divine,
Beyond the reaches of this darkened land.
So in this realm where shadows reign supreme,
Exists a difference, though it may seem slight.
It lies in whether one's soul shall dream,
And escape this world, bathed in endless night.
For if one chooses to ignite that spark,
To nurture hope and brave despair's abyss,
The difference lies within a fire's arc
To pull them free from darkness' gnarled twist.

XIV

Futile Fragility

In fleeting moments, life's fragile embrace,
A delicate dance upon a razor's edge.
A breath, a heartbeat, a wisp of grace
, All can vanish, leaving an empty pledge.
The specter of fate, an unrelenting force,
Mocks our illusions of permanence and might.
In an instant, dreams shatter without remorse,
Leaving shattered hopes in the cold, dark night.
What once seemed steadfast, now crumbles to dust,
The fragile vessel of life, a fleeting wisp.
In the blink of an eye, all turns to rust,
Leaving us grasping at shadows, a futile grasp.
So cherish each moment's breath,
For life's fragile beauty is touched by death.

XV

Paradox

Alas, the world, a tapestry of darkness woven with threads of irony,
where light is but a fleeting illusion, a cruel jest played upon the
stage of existence.
Behold this paradox, where the very essence of life is steeped in
shadows,
where hope is but a fragile ember flickering in the engulfing night.
In this labyrinth of paradoxes, the world parades its hypocrisy,
adorning itself with the masquerade of benevolence
while concealing the venomous fangs of malevolence.
How ironic it is that in the pursuit of progress, we sow the seeds of
destruction,
nurturing the fruits of our own demise.
The symphony of dissonance resounds, as harmony eludes our grasp,
and chaos reigns supreme.

The irony of this world lies in its propensity to extinguish the
flickering flames
of innocence, to taint the pure with the stain of corruption.
And in the cacophony of suffering, we seek solace in the arms of
empathy,

only to be met with apathy and indifference.
How bitterly ironic that in our quest for connection,
we find ourselves adrift in a sea of isolation.

The very fabric of this world is woven
with the threads of contradiction, where love is tainted by betrayal,
where virtue is overshadowed by vice.

We strive for meaning in a world steeped in absurdity,
yearning for purpose while drifting in the chaos of existence.

Irony, like a mocking specter, haunts our every endeavor
, turning triumph into tragedy and joy into sorrow.

So here I stand, wandering the ruins of shattered illusions,
bearing witness to the darkness that cloaks this world in its embrace.
For in the heart of this dissonance
, I find a perverse kind of truth – that the world's irony is the very
essence of its being,
a reflection of our own flawed nature,
an eternal dance of light and shadow,
hope and despair, life and death.

XVI

Cacophony

Alongside the deadline's dread, a chaotic boom echoes,
Shattering the silence, stirring the shallow depths,
Instigating a dance of discord in the dirt,
Where children cower, their innocence creeping away.
The cacophony of chaos, a cruel crescendo,
As shadows deepen and despair descends,
The dirt suffused with darkness, a sinister symphony,
Instigating fear in the hearts of the innocent.
In the shallow graves of hope, dreams lie dormant,
As the deadline looms, a relentless specter,
Children's laughter silenced, their spirits in shadow,
Creeping through the chaos, seeking solace in vain.

XVII

Forbidden Wealth

In the depths of time, a group of treasure hunters set sail,
their eager hearts beating like the rhythmic pulse of the waves
crashing against the ancient shore.
They sought the fabled artifact,
whispered to possess the power to bestow untold riches upon its
possessor.
Their journey echoed with the creaking of the timbers,
the billowing of sails, and the murmuring of the restless sea,
a symphony of anticipation and fervent whispers.

As they ventured deeper into the uncharted realm,
their footsteps echoed through the labyrinthine corridors of the
forgotten ruins,
their voices reverberating off the moss-covered walls like a haunting
melody.
The air hummed with the promise of untold fortune,
a siren's song that beckoned them deeper into the darkness,
their greed mounting like a tempest on the horizon.

At last, they uncovered the artifact, a gleaming relic
adorned with intricate carvings that seemed to whisper tales of for-
gotten empires and lost treasures. The hunters' gasps of awe mingled
with the metallic clink of their tools as they pried it from
Its ancient resting place, setting off a chain of events
that would reverberate with ominous resonance.
With each passing day, the artifact's allure grew, casting a spell
over the once-rational minds of the hunters.
Their voices rose in fevered arguments, the harsh consonants
clashing like thunder in the encroaching storm.
The artifact's presence seemed to fill the air with a low, pulsat-
ing hum,
a dissonant melody that gnawed at their sanity, driving them to the
brink of obsession.
The treasure hunters, consumed by avarice, turned against each
other,
their greed manifesting in the sharp clang of blades and the guttural
cries of betrayal.
Madness seeped into their souls like a poison,
the once harmonious camaraderie now a cacophony of discordant
desires and shattered trust.
As the curse tightened its grip,
the hunters' minds became a tumultuous sea of conflicting emotions,
their laughter a chilling echo of derangement,
their whispers a maddening chorus of desperation.
The artifact, now a beacon of their downfall, pulsed
with an otherworldly resonance, its insidious song drowning
out the last vestiges of reason.
In the end, the treasure hunters succumbed
to the artifact's malevolent influence,
their once vibrant spirits reduced to hollow echoes of their former
selves.
The cursed relic, now a silent sentinel lost within the ruins, bore
witness to the tragic symphony of avarice and madness,

a haunting testament to the folly
of those who seek to grasp the forbidden fruits of untold wealth.

XVIII

Theater of Absurdity

In the heart of the city, where lights gleam and shadows linger,
A symphony of sirens pierces the night, a haunting serenade,
Where dreams are devoured by the relentless jaws of ambition,
And the pursuit of happiness is a cruel illusion, a masquerade of despair.
Among the towering spires and bustling streets, humanity thrives and withers,
A paradox of existence, where joy and sorrow entwine like lovers in an eternal embrace,

Where the wealthy languish in the poverty of their own avarice,
And the destitute find solace in the richness of their shattered spirits.
In this labyrinth of paradox, where laughter mingles with tears,
The jesters wear crowns, and the kings bow in jest,

Where love is a thorn, and pain a tender caress,
And the pursuit of joy leads to the depths of despair.
The righteous stumble, ensnared by their own virtue,
As the wicked thrive in the shadows they cast,
For the scales of justice tilt with capricious whim,

And fate weaves a tapestry of cruel paradox.
In the grand theater of life, where tragedies unfold,
The actors are but pawns in fate's relentless game,
Where the audience applauds the folly of mortal hearts,
And the playwright revels in the irony of existence.
So we navigate the corridors of our own absurdity,
Embracing the paradox that colors our journey,
For in the heart of darkness, a glimmer of truth,
That within the dissonance, we find our fragile dance.

XIX

Revelations of the Raven

In the shadows of the night, where stars refuse to shine,
A raven's caw breaks the stillness, a creature so divine.
From its ebony feathers, secrets it does hold,
Whispering of mystic omens, of stories yet untold.

A reverie it weaves, as moonlight casts its spell,
Unveiling revelations that the night's darkness does compel.
In the realm of midnight, where dreams and nightmares meet,
Behold the wondrous tapestry of secrets so discreet.

Beneath the cloak of the heavens, darkened skies prevail,
Stars no longer shimmer, for secrets now set sail.
With every flicker of their light, tales of old are spun,
Etching tales of forgotten lore, till morning's first begun.

Mystical omens dance through the whispers of the wind,
Their cryptic messages unfurl, where shadows gently rend.
The moon, a silver crescent, illuminates the way,
Leading to mysterious places, where truth and fable sway.
Within this realm of secrets, where mortals rarely tread,

Lies a sanctuary for the lost, where darkened souls are led.
Through labyrinthine pathways, of moonlit midnight's call,
Echo ancient tales of sorrow, of love's eternal thrall.

Revelations, dark and deep, emerge from hidden depths,
Their words, a symphony of truth, the melody unkept.
For within the Raven's reverie, answers there may lie,
To questions long unanswered, beneath the starlit sky.

A tapestry of shadows, upon which stories reside,
Woven by forgotten whispers, where secrets now reside.
The raven, silent sentinel of the midnight hour's embrace,
Transcends the borders of reality, unveiling hidden grace.

Through tales of ancient mystics, whispers of the twilight,
The Raven's midnight reverie unlocks gates of insight.
Each feather in its being, a key to worlds unseen,
Revealing secrets long forgotten, beneath the midnight sheen.
So explore this realm of secrets, within the raven's gaze,
Embrace the darkened skies, where mysteries always graze.
For in the tales of midnight, lies the truth we long to find,
Locked away within the depths of our veiled human mind.

XX

Empire of Ash

It was a pleasure to burn, in fires untamed,
A sinister delight, where darkness remained,
To witness things devoured, by flames ruthless and wild,
To relish in destruction, to consume like a child.
The fervent blaze dancing, a malevolent sight,
As it swallowed the world, with an insatiable appetite,
A special pleasure it was, to see life's demise, T
o witness its agonized wails, its desperate cries.

Oh, the ecstasy derived, from the scorching heat,
A sadistic thirst, none could defeat,
To see beauty crumble, as ashes took flight,
Transforming all in its path, to a desolate night.

The grandeur of forests, once lush and alive,
Reduced to embers, as flames would thrive,
Leaves turned to cinders, like dreams torn apart,
Within this abyss, cruelty found its own art.

Majestic buildings, once symbols of might,

Reduced to ruins, haunted by the night,
Smoke veiled the heavens and choked out the sun,
A world torn asunder, in chaos overrun.
For the flames knew no mercy, no fleeting remorse,
They reveled in torment, with no guiding force,
In their fiery embrace, innocence was slain,
And sanity decayed, surrendering to the flame.

Oh, the rivers that flowed, now a liquid inferno,
Bodies consumed, in a torment eternal,
The scent of charred flesh, an unholy perfume,
As life's vibrant colors turned to shades of doom.

And as the night deepened, a foreboding gloom fell,
An odious presence, insidious and cruel spell,
For the fire whispered secrets, only darkness would know,
Promising empires of ashes, where torment would grow.
The sky, once adorned with stars shining bright,
Now cloaked in shadows, with utmost delight,
The moon bowed in sorrow, veiled by despair,
As the flames of destruction, consumed the night air.

XXI

Slaughterhouse

At 7:00 PM the abattoir awakes,
Its gates creak open, shadows cast by stakes,
The enchanted hour, when life takes its toll,
Where the innocence of flesh is bought and sold.
The air is dense with secrets and despair,
As the slaughtered souls whisper tales of their affair,
Within its walls, a symphony of death unfolds,
Harvesting silence, as destiny takes hold.

With each swing of the blade, a heartbeat departs,
The echoes of life fade into the dark arts,
Serrated knives pierce the veil of existence,
Blood, the ink that stains this somber existence.
Lamentations linger within the cold floors,
Muffled cries, amid the deafening roars,
Their pleading eyes meet the indifferent gaze,
A tragic dance, where death and life amaze.
The liquid ruby flows, its path is clear,
A river of crimson, a testament of fear,
The walls bear witness to this macabre stage,

Where fragility meets the world's merciless rage.
The butcher, a conductor, in bloody attire,
Wields his instrument, fueling the pyre,
Skin meets the touch of the unforgiving steel,
As life parts ways, consumed by his zeal.
The chorus of the abattoir sings its refrain,
The agonized notes escaping each vein,
While the aroma of flesh dances with the breeze,
As the symphony's crescendo reaches its seize.
The clock ticks, relentless, as night turns to morn,
The abattoir rests, weary, its purpose now torn,
For in life's grand tapestry, such roles do exist,
We're both the butchers and the ones who resist.

XXII

Ethereal Resplendence

In the depths of night's ebony shroud,
Where shadows writhe like tendrils, proud,
Emerges a symphony, a cosmic affair,
That only few mortals have a chance to share.
Beneath a lunar gaze, a velvet stage,
Is set for the dance of firefly's engage,
A waltz among the stars, a nocturnal ballet,
Where luminescent creatures come to play.
Like clusters of stardust flung from above,
These tiny dancers possess a light, like love.
With ethereal glow, they illuminate my sight,
Fluttering and pirouetting, a magical invite.

They emerge from the whispers of darkness profound,
Tiny beacons of hope, floating all around,
In their radiant brilliance, secrets they unveil,
Leaving me enraptured, breathless and frail.
A thousand delicate wings, flickering and bright,
Paint the canvas of night with purest delight,
Guided by ancestral knowledge they possess,

Binding their flight with nature's caress.
Their choreography, a mystical flight,
Entwines hearts and souls, embracing the night,
They sway to the rhythm of the celestial score,
Intricate patterns, forever craving more.
As gentle zephyrs whisper lullabies,
Their glow multiplies, weaves a tapestry of sighs,
I watch in awe, spellbound, as if upon a stage,
Fiery sparks of life dancing in a boundless rage.
Their grace flickers like forgotten dreams,
Bathing the night in their luminous beams,
Uncountable threads weave a celestial tapestry,
Entangling my emotions, awestruck and free.
With each pulsating breath, they banish the gloom,
An enchantment they bring, dispelling all doom,
In their radiant presence, worries they defy,
Transforming darkness into a starlit sky.
The cosmos rejoices at their celestial ballet,
Moonbeams applaud, the night turns into day,
An orchestra of fireflies, glimmers of delight,
That banish despair, igniting hope's bright light.
Yet, like all fleeting wonders, this dance shall cease,
As the night fades away, leaving echoes of peace,
But the firefly's magic lingers, forever aglow,
Etched in my memory, an everlasting show.

XXIII

Midnight

In the darkest hour, where shadows creep,
Midnight confides in the silent moon's keep.
A secret pact they share, with none to declare,
Unveiling tales shrouded in deepest despair.
When weary souls rest in the webs where dreams untold,
Midnight unravels in its enigmatic fold.
Like a sable blanket draped over the earth,
Obsidian whispers echo with eerie mirth.
A moonbeam casts its pallid, somber glow,
Revealing secrets unspoken, woven with woe.
Drenched in darkness, where secrets convene,
Midnight confides, embracing the unseen.
What does the clock's hand conceal under the weight,
Of timeless hours ebbing, in grim fate's gait?
Midnight sighs heavy, sorrows locked in its core,
Enigmatic musings dance on the darkened floor.
The moon, a guardian etched in celestial grace,
Lends an ear to Midnight, embracing its chase.
A tale of souls lost in the labyrinth of night,
Unveiling the shadows that shroud their plight.

The moon glimmers, a beacon of borrowed light,
Illuminating Midnight's depths with icy insight.
For the moon bears witness, a silent confidante,
To secrets spun from sorrow's fragile enchant.
Uncharted realms collide in Midnight's embrace,
The moonlights on the melancholy's traced face
What tides of torment surge beneath the guise,
Of the midnight hour's haunting disguise?

XXIV

Invitation//The Cell

Come into my cell, where shadows reside,
Within these haunting walls, both dread and pride.
Make yourself at home, a guest of the night,
Here darkness reigns supreme, obscuring all light.
Beware, dear visitor, this somber embrace,
For here lies a tale, laced with sorrow and grace.
Through these forbidden realms, let me guide,
Untangling the secrets, none should dare abide.
In each whispered word, hear a plea for release,
From this eternal torment, seeking inner peace.
Here, embodied darkness finds its forlorn voice,
Through echoes of anguish, secrets to rejoice.
Come into my cell, make yourself at home,
In this humble refuge, where shadows roam.
Seek solace among the darkness,
find respite in the gloom,

For within these worn walls, there lies a tale,
The hisses of a Gorgon, her gaze casting a petrifying spell,
Where once beauty thrived, only horror now fell.

Her wretched curse, a burden she bore,
Turning all who beheld her into stone evermore.
Here, whispers echo from the long-forgotten past,
Of dreams that faded, things never meant to last.

Each crack is a testament, a lesson to be learned,
For every scar is a symbol, each scar is a page turned.
But heed the warning, as you delve in the pointless cries,
For this tale can consume you, where hope slowly dies.
Within my solemn walls, linger these stories untold,
Come into my cell, but do not let yourself be controlled.

XXV

Opening the Door

Each night, as twilight weaves its spell upon the weary sky,
We gaze into the glass, seeking reflections where wonders lie.
Oh, dearest traveler of thine own fragile reality,
Envision what may lie beyond, in boundless duality.
The mirrors, beholders of secrets buried deep within,
Their slick surfaces a portal, tempting us to step in.
What worlds await us in those realms opaque,
Where chaos and harmony intertwine, and dreams are born to break?
Behind the silvered veils, corridors of labyrinthine nature

Parallel worlds awaken, each with its own unique stature.
In one, the skies are eternally laden with gloom and despair,
And the sun, a mere illusion, glitched in a perpetual snare.
There, the shadows rule, their ancient empire vast,
Manifesting tortured echoes from forgotten past.
The denizens, ghastly visages shrouded in distress,
With vacant eyes so hollow, souls dwelling in duress.

In another world, a utopia bathed in ethereal light,
Where seraphic beings soar, transcending mortal sight.

Celestial melodies from unseen harmonies resound,
And tendrils of joy embrace all they surround.
Within the mirrors' grasp, forged pathways to enigma,
Their tapestries woven with threads both twisted and true,

Unveiling glimpses beyond the curtain that divides me from you.
Each realm, a phantasmagoric reflection, shifting hues at the seams,
Where the consequences of our choices, the stuff of fevered dreams.
But defying the siren call of mirrored dimensions,
Is a wisdom bestowed on cursed souls, and laden with intentions.

For to enter such domains, the price oft unseen,
A fragment of thy soul, forever tethered between.
A labyrinth of decisions, evermore to contend,
What once begun, a destiny's journey with no amend.
So here we stand, contemplating what lies beyond the pane,
Ensnared within the tapestry of our choices, bound by the chain.

The mirrors, mere portals, seductive in their arcane allure,
Beckoning us gently, a call few could endure.
Yet, somber musings persist, as the midnight hour we keep,
For what if the reflection is not one of sight but of sleep?
What if our world is but a twisted counterpart to what lies afar,
And in this darkness, we are the portals, as we've opened the
door ajar?

XXVI

Refrain of the Cosmos

Fiery travelers blaze with celestial might.
Across the vast expanse of space they soar,
Leaving behind a trail of cosmic lore.

Oh, how they dance, those burning stars,
Guiding lost souls from afar.
Their restless journey through the skies,

Reveals omens, secrets, and mystic ties.
The moon, a melancholic mistress, she weeps,
As she watches the world below, shrouded in sleep.

Her tears fall like silver laden with sorrow,
Whispering tales of a bleak tomorrow.
From distant galaxies with unfathomable histories,

The travelers bring warnings and apocalyptic mysteries.
They speak of ancient gods entwined in starry realms,
And of cosmic battles fought with celestial helms.

Fiery meteors crash upon the desolate land,
Leaving scars upon the Earth's outstretched hand.
Their impact echoes, like a mourning cry,

As the world succumbs to its impending demise.
But swirling inside the chaos, there exists a yearning,
A flicker of hope, unyielding and burning.

From the ashes of destruction, new life springs,
As nature fights back and the cosmos sings.
Yet, the tales from the cosmos remain,

Whispered by the stars in a chilling refrain.
They foretell of worlds unspoken, unseen,
Where darkness reigns, and light is but a dream.

In this long and dark symphony of the universe,
Fiery travelers bear witness, a solemn curse.
Within their celestial wanderings, they confide,

The secrets of existence, both cruel and wide.
So, in the blackest night, I gaze up high, seeking solace beneath
the sky.
For in the fiery travelers' tales, I find a song of the cosmos, forever
entwined.

XXVII

Black Lilac

In a chamber of rhythmic whispers,
Where shadows embraced the night,
There intertwined the dreams of dancers,
In a symphony of graceful flight.
A pitch-black room, devoid of light,
Where souls ignited timeless tunes,
On hallowed ground they found respite,
As bodies swayed like gentle dunes.
Within this hushed and secret space,
Where darkness spawned a mystic spell,
Ebon threads spun through the maze,
And stories of silken footsteps fell.
The air, it clung with fragrant grace,
As lilacs bloomed and notes entwined,
Their scent, celestial, filled the space,
Transporting minds to realms unconfined.

Like sable feathers on a midnight breeze,
The murmurs of melodies unfurled,
Embracing minds with whispered ease,

As dancers wove their tales, unfurled.
Each motion painted infinite lines,
In this pitch-black chamber they beheld,
With closed eyes, delicate designs,
A dance through realms where stories dwelled.
An ethereal waltz in the night's abyss,
A grand pas de deux 'neath moonlit gleam,
Twirling and twining through the void's kiss,
Revealing secrets yet to be seen.
Oh, the lilacs' fragrance ever so sweet,
The symphony of steps hidden from sight,
Where dancers' hearts and rhythms meet,
In that pitch-black room, eternal delight.

And as the night wore on, they waltzed,
In harmony with the lilacs' perfume,
Through pitch-black depths their bodies exalted,
Till dawn reclaimed the room.
Yet secrets lingered in the air,
Of dancers lost within the gloom,
Forever captured, forever ensnared,
In that pitch-black room.
So let the lilacs bloom with pride,
As dancers take their glorious flight,
In pitch-black chambers, worlds collide,
Guided by fragrance and absence of light.

XXVIII

The Box

In a hidden corner of time's domain,
Lies a secret box, a treasure's bane,
Wrapped in whispers of tales untold,
Its key guarded by secrets and mold.
A veil woven from a velvet ribbon
No mortal eye has ever gazed,
Upon the marvels this box embraced.
Within its hallowed, timber womb,
Lay wonders shrouded in endless gloom,
A symphony of enigma and surprise,
Awaiting the seeker with curious eyes.

Each turn of the key, a whispered plea,
Unleashes ancient tales, wild and free,
From realms unknown, they come alive,
Inspiring wonder, like bees to a hive.
And deep inside this sacred vault,
A curious ice cube tray is caught,
Frozen moments, trapped in time,
Captivating, in their frozen prime.

Each indentation, a memory's hold,
Of laughter, strife, stories untold,
Through countless seasons, they remain,
Frozen souvenirs, they shall not wane.

A secret romance, a stolen kiss,
Or heartbreak's grip, an icy abyss,
The embodiment of life's refrain,
A tangible echo of joy and pain.
This secret box, bridging past and now,
Holds memories, like a precious vow,
Unraveling the tapestry of a thousand lives,
Binding dreams and whispers that survive.
Within this box, time's essence resides,
Where past, present, and future coincides,
Veiled by a ribbon, soft and profound,
A tale for the seeker; but not easily found.

XXIX

Into the Night

With a pinprick of pain, a voodoo doll rests its head,
In a realm of despair, where life's hope had fled.
Crafted with care in a sinister design,
Each stitch whispers of torment, a dark art refined.
With every malicious thrust, a victim's fate is sealed,
Their essence trapped within, a destiny concealed.
A puppeteer wickedly tugs at heartstrings,
As the voodoo doll dances to the tune darkness sings.
A lone balloon drifts through the murky night sky,
Its fragile facade masking secrets held high.
Silent screams, echoes of anguish, it carries within,
Inflated with despair, a testament to sin.
Through twisted alleys and forgotten streets,
It floats, an omen of silence, where despair retreats.
A prisoner of sorrow, encased by thin air,
The balloon seeks release from its soul's endless snare.
Where tendrils of smoke intertwine and unwind,
A tale of lost souls emerges, the twisted kind.
Whispering tendrils coil, concealing secrets in the haze,
Haunted wisps of secrets drifting through a suffocating maze.

Within this ethereal labyrinth, phantoms come alive,
A swirling dance of despair, where sorrows thrive.
Their cries emerge from the encircling fog,
A spectral symphony, mournful notes inquire and jog.
And there, in the heart of the smoke, a keyhole peers,
A gateway to the unknown, where trepidation steers.
Unseen eyes observing, secrets waiting to be revealed,
Infinite possibilities, obscured, yet concealed.
Echoes of lost souls linger, yearning to escape,
Every sorrowful tale, every anguished scrape.
Locked behind the keyhole, destiny held tight,
Awaiting the courage to venture into the night.

XXX

Concealed by the Fog

What stories does the fog conceal?
Those tales whispered by the elusive mist,
As it weaves its way through time and space,
Hiding secrets in its translucent embrace.

The mist dances upon abandoned streets,
Lingering in corners where shadows meet.
It paints a hazy veil over the past,
A tapestry of memories that won't last.

In the morning hours, as dawn awakes,
It wraps the world in its ethereal stakes.
Obstructing views with a mystical shroud,
Leaving riddles in the minds of the crowd.

Through wisps of smoke,
I glimpse the ghostly past,
A reflection of moments that couldn't last.
Muted figures cross my line of sight,
Their stories woven in the fog's delight.

I peer through the misted windows with care,
Seeking remnants of lives trapped in the air.
What tales lie hidden behind the glass?
Of love unrequited or dreams that would pass?

A dilapidated building stands tall,
Its windows clouded, revealing no thrall.
What whispers haunt those forsaken halls?
Of laughter echoing in empty walls?

As twilight descends, the mist grows thicker,
Enveloping the landscape like a silent ticker.
I tread through foggy landscapes of old,
Diving into memories yet untold.

In ancient libraries, where books decay,
The fog gathers thick, obscuring the way.
But in this haze, secrets start to unveil
, As whispers from forgotten manuscripts sail.

I lose myself in the mysteries of time,
Every step forging a forgotten rhyme.
The mist guides me through a labyrinth maze,
Revealing stories in its mystical haze.

But as the night deepens, the fog grows dense,
Muting the world with its solemn pretense.
What stories lie beneath this thickened cloak?
Legends fading into the shadows and smoke.

The misty memoirs of long-lost yesteryears,
Devoured by time, like a river of tears.
They beckon and haunt with every passing breath,

Drawing me closer to their impending death.

So, I surrender to the fog's enchanting spell,
Immersing myself in the stories it will tell.
For in this misted world, alive with lore,
I find solace, as history I explore.
What tales does the fog conceal within?
Of love, loss, or battles none could win?
I pause, listening to the fog's solemn sighs,
Knowing it guards the truth, hidden in disguise.

XXXI

The Phoenix's Pyre

A being that rises from ashes of fiery light.
Glorious and resplendent, its feathers aflame,
The mighty Phoenix, its destiny to claim,
From the fiery depths it emerges anew
, A symbol of rebirth and cycles we pursue.

Born in ancient times, this wondrous bird,
Its existence, by mortals, its tale unheard,
Yet their longing for renewal and flame's embrace,
Mirrors its essence, a mythical grace.

From darkness it rises, dancing in the sky,
Igniting the heavens with its fiery cry,
It soars with purpose, through celestial lanes,
Igniting hope and vanquishing domains.
In flames it perishes, consumed by desire,
Its demise, but the start of its fervent fire
For deep within the embers of ash and pain,
Lies resurrection, a chant it shall regain.
From the ashes it emerges, with newfound strength

, A creature reborn, as life's cycles extend,
Resplendent wings unfurl, alight with fervor,
Symbolic of perseverance, forever.
It teaches us that through trials we grow,
That we must embrace change, let our spirits flow,
For just as the Phoenix faces the flame,
We too must face darkness to ignite our aim.
Beneath the radiant sun, it glows with might,
A beacon of hope, a celestial light,
Its cycle eternal, a mirage sublime,
A reminder of the passage of time.
Through centuries and eons, its story's passed,
From ancient realms to futures vast,
For every life, a tale to aspire,
Of rebirth, renewal, and ancient fire.

Forsaken Moments

In a place where time hath whispered its tale,
Where once stood tall, now stands a restless wail,
A forgotten structure, a silent grove,
An old, dilapidated barn, dreams once behoove.
Its wooden frame, weary beneath the weeds,
With stories etched upon its weathered beads,
Through thunderous storms and winters fierce,
This barn endured, a fortress to appease.
Now, alas, a caved-in roof, a bowed head,
Once embraced the sky, where sunlight led,
As moonbeams danced upon its homey floor,
Now shadows linger, a place to explore.
Within these walls, where laughter used to ring,
And children danced with wild flowers, in spring,
A symphony of life, once echoed so grand,
Now lies in shambles, a relic, unplanned.

The wind, a melodic mourner, through cracks it seeps,
Sighing the secrets which time no longer keeps,
From fractured rafters, an elegy it sings,

For the barn that once stood proud, with hope-filled wings.
With each passing day, its walls grow frail,
The touch of decay, its somber tale,
Once painted red, now a canvas of decay,
The colors peeling, fading into disarray.
The scent of hay, a whisper lost among the dust,
The songs of swallows, replaced with solemn rust,
Windows, once gleaming with stories amassed,
Cracked and shattered, gazing upon the past.
Through broken panes, sunlight weeps with remorse,
Casting shadows, revealing this aged discourse,
Where beams of light and darkness interweave,
A dance of forgotten memories, yet to retrieve
.And as the years pass, and seasons come and go,
The old barn's spirit, never ceases to grow,
A sanctuary for souls seeking solace and rest,
For within its decaying walls, nostalgia is blessed.
So, when you come across an old, decrepit sight,
A barn, forgotten, battling against its silent plight,
Remember the tales that whisper in the wind,
For it's those forsaken moments that lie deep within.

XXXIII

Terror From The Skies

A spiraling juggernaut, a terror from the skies,
A force that brings destruction, a tempest that defies.

Awakening from slumber, as the morning sun does rise,
The day begins for this fierce creature, relentless in the skies.

A tornado, birthed from fury, roams with purpose proud,
A creature born of cyclone, a tempest fierce and loud.

With a roar, the tempest rises, the tempest spreads its wings,
The shrieking voices of the wind, the chorus that it sings.

It rips through the tranquil air, with thunder's war-drums loud,
A symphony of chaos, billowing dark storm clouds.

The atmosphere turns sickly, a bile-green sky does loom,
As swirling winds grow stronger, foretelling of the gloom.

Blinding lightning slices through, a vengeful silver lance,

Illuminating the destruction, swallowed in its mighty dance.

Hailstones, large as apples, are flung with deadly pride,
A merciless assault upon all things that dare reside.

From rooftops to the meadows, the tempest's hands doth rake,
Crushing all beneath its might, causing the earth to quake.

Invisible it may appear, a phantom, void of grace,
But like a colossus rages, with its havoc interlaced.

And as the day progresses, the tempest does not rest,
It ravages and it conquers, despoiling with no jest.
The rain pours down in torrents, like lashes from the sky,
A deluge, never-ending, as the tempest's echoes cry.

Endlessly it lashes out, in torrents, rivers flow,
Creating floods from the heavens, where once was earth below.

Sirens wail their mournful songs, howling through the night,
A warning to all who dare to face this fearsome sight.

The echoes of the siren's wail, the tempest's vicious moan,
Are joined by phantom dust clouds, the tempest's reign is shown.

From broken dreams and shattered hopes, it rises from the midst,
In twisting gusts and ferocious winds, the tempest does persist

. Ancestral whispers haunt its core, a legacy to bear,
As it paints a path of devastation, without a thought or care.
And then, as night falls gently, soothing the land so vast,
This monster of destruction, its fury quelled at last.

Alone once more, it slumbers, within the depths of night,

Leaving behind its trail of ruin, hidden from the light.

XXXIV

Abyss Within

In darkness deep, where shadows creep,
A terror lurks, it preys on sleep.
A suffocating, crushing weight,
Claustrophobia, an unyielding fate.
In narrow halls, I find no ease,
A constricting grip, it aims to seize.
The walls draw near, they mock and jeer,
My frantic heart, consumed by fear.
In whispered breaths, the walls confide,
Their secrets dark, they seek to hide.
Their closeness suffocates my soul,
And through my mind, the panic rolls.
The air grows thin, I cannot breathe,
A choking grip, I cannot leave.
Echoes of dread, they pierce my mind,
In this confinement, I am confined.

The flickering light, a cruel charade,
In shifting shadows, my mind's betrayed.
They twist and turn, a haunting waltz,

In this abyss, I pay the cost
I long to break free, to see the sky,
To feel the open space, to breathe, to fly.
But in this darkness, I am confined,
By walls that bind, and thoughts unkind.

I fight the panic, I fight the dread,
But in this darkness, I feel I'm led.
Led to madness, led to despair,
In the grip of claustrophobia's snare.
My mind a prison, my thoughts a cage,
Trapped in this torment, consumed by rage.
I scream for release, but none can hear

XXXV

The Dancing Dragon's Lullaby

In realms beyond the waking hour, where dreams take flight,
There dwells a creature mystical, igniting pure delight,
With scales as iridescent as the moonlit night,
Behold the wondrous marvel, the dancing dragon bright.
Its eyes, twin orbs of serpentine allure,
Reflect the promise of a world beyond the obscure,
A fire burns within, an ember's vibrant glow,
Guiding its graceful steps, where life's rhythms flow.
From Eastern shores it first emerged with grace untold,
An elegant creature, captivating, in a dance unfold,
Its body twists and turns, a silken ribbon in the wind,
Fueling dreams and hopes within the minds of those pinned.
With every movement, songs of ancient lore resound,
Carried by the wings that lift it from the ground,
A melody of passion, a symphony of ancient tales,
Drawing souls together, as each heartbeat pales.

The earth beneath it trembles; flames ignite the sky,

Its fiery breath a testament to spirits truly high,
In every leap and bound, the world begins to see,
The power and the beauty of this dragon, wild and free.
With nimble steps, it weaves enchantment in the air,
A tapestry of motion, divinely crafted fair,
The shadows dance alongside, as if they've come alive,
In awe, the world takes notice, succumbing to the drive.

Through crowded streets and bustling markets, it traverses,
A beacon of excitement, where wonder never ceases,
The people, young and aged alike, forget their daily strife,
As they join the cosmic rhythm in the dance of life.
Through verdant valleys, and atop the highest hills,
The dragon finds its canvas, where grace and passion thrills

Silent whispers fill the air, a hush of sheer delight,
As nature's creatures gather to witness this majestic sight.
So, let us raise our voices, in honor of this being,
A creature of pure beauty, forever worth esteeming,
And when you close your eyes tonight, in slumber's calm embrace,
Imagine the dancing dragon's grace

XXXVI

The Unseen Palette

In the stillness of the night, shadows dance,
A world of hues unseen, a spectral trance.
They whisper tales of sorrow and woe,
In the depths where colors ebb and flow.
A mournful melody fills the air,
As the veil of twilight begins to tear.
The fading light weeps its final song,
A requiem for the day, now gone.
In the heart of darkness, a silent plea,
A solitary figure yearning to be free.
Enshrouded in the cloak of the unseen,
A soul adrift in a world, serene.
A yearning for warmth, a touch so tender,
In the hidden spectrum, emotions surrender.
The ache of a heart, a love untold,
In the depths of the unseen, it unfolds.
In the hidden canvas, memories reside,
A tapestry of moments, where secrets hide.
Each stroke and swirl, a story untold,
In the depths of the unseen, it unfolds.

A heavy burden, a darkness so profound,
In the realm of colors, an absence is found.
A weight that crushes, a soul so frail,
In the depths of the unseen, it sets its sail.
In the silence, a longing for light,
To pierce the darkness, to banish the night.
A yearning for hues that once did gleam,
In the depths of the unseen, a fervent dream
Though hidden from sight, their presence strong,
In the world of shadows, they still belong.
An unseen palette, a symphony of grace,
In the depths of the unseen, they find their place.

XXXVII

Null

I am nothing.
In the heart of the cosmic abyss,
Where light and time cease to exist,
A voracious maw devours all,
An infinite void, an ethereal sprawl.

A celestial anomaly, a cosmic scar,
It bends and warps, it devours from afar.
A boundary where laws are defied,
In the depths of darkness, all is nullified.

Eternal silence, a vacuum vast,
A realm of nothingness, where time is cast.
Into the abyss, a descent so deep,
Where galaxies perish, and stars do weep.

A singularity, a point of no return,
Where matter is crushed, and souls do burn.
A gravitational grip, an unyielding embrace,
In the heart of nothing, no trace of grace.

A cosmic enigma, a riddle unsolved,
It beckons with whispers, a mystery evolved.
A shroud of darkness, an enigmatic call,
In the depths of nothing, where echoes stall.

A distortion of reality, a fabric torn,
In the presence of nothing, all is unborn.
A dance of shadows, a spectral ballet,
In the embrace of nothing, all colors fray.

A tapestry of stars, a canvas so vast,
In the pull of nothing, they vanish fast.
A symphony of silence, a haunting song,
In the depths of nothing, where echoes prolong.

In the cosmic dance, where chaos reigns,
In the grip of nothing, where all refrains.
An existential void, a philosophical blight,
In the embrace of nothing, where all takes flight.

A testament to absence, a void so stark,
In the presence of nothing, all is marked.
A specter of oblivion, a chasm profound,
In the heart of nothing, where all is unbound.

A swirling vortex, a celestial dance,
In the maw of nothing, all find no chance.
A cosmic expanse, a mysterious shroud,
In the depths of nothing, all is avowed.

In the heart of the cosmic abyss,
Where light and time cease to exist,
I am nothing, and in nothing I dwell,

In the depths of the void, where all is farewell.

THE SECRET CONVERSATIONS OF FLOWERS

In the twilight's hush, where moonbeams softly play,
the flowers gather 'neath the stars' beguiling sway.
Their petals shimmer with a spectral glow,
as they murmur secrets in the language only they know.
Shivering in the evening's chill, the
Windflowers' delicate blooms seem to tremble still,
speaking of the ancient tales they've heard,
of lost loves and dreams that never stirred.

Weaving enchanting stories in the dead of night,
the Moonlilies ponder the mysteries of the universe's design
and the fleeting nature of mortal time with their pale, ghostly light.

Chanting haunting laments, old as time's debut, the
Nightshades mourn the passing of forgotten days
and the souls lost in life's intricate maze with their somber, sable hue.
Conspiring in whispers of impending harm, the
Belladonnas ponder the depths of human desire
and the allure of temptation's treacherous fire
with their poisonous charm.

Spinning tales of realms beyond mortal care,
the Ghost Orchids speak of phantoms and spectral wraiths,
lost souls wandering in twilight's waning baths, ethereal and rare.
Shrouded in mystery's veil, the Black Roses
whisper of love and sorrow, and the toll of betrayal,
pondering the shadows that dance in the night
and the secrets hidden from mortal sight.
In this enigmatic garden where the flowers convene,
a blooming symphony of secrets unseen, unfurling

their petals to reveal their clandestine lore in this
whimsical dance of darkness and allure.
So heed the tales of these spectral blooms, for in their whispers,
the garden's mystery looms, enchanting and tranquil
in the moonlit hours when the world is still.

XXXVIII

Let The Rain Fall

From heavens high, clouds pregnant with strife,
An orchestra of thunder, drums of life,
Resonating cries, that pierce the air,
As tempest's fury turns skies unfair.
Within droplets that form, a tale they hold,
Of sorrow's tears, of secrets untold,
They gather strength, in heaven's shroud,
As darkness descends in clamorous cloud.
Like spectral messengers of woe,
They gather momentum, their purpose to bestow,
With every gust, the storm unfurls,
A torrential symphony, their song of the world.
The thrill that courses, from cloud to earth,
A celestial journey, of chaos and rebirth,
They tumble and crash, upon the land,
Cleansing the scars with a tender hand.
In the realm where night forever reigns,
Where moonlight, too, remains in chains,
The raindrops fall, never to cease,

A darkened lullaby, a mournful peace.
Each drop holds a tale, a whispered secret,
From clouds that mourn, they softly emit,
A requiem for dreams forever dashed,
For hopes eroded, and loves trashed.

They cascade down like silver tears,
Washing away the burden, erasing fears
, For in their depths, lies a gentle might,
To heal the wounds of the darkest night.
Through cracked windows, they silently creep,

Drenching the world, in a watery deep,
They tap, tap, tap, on weary shoulders,
Awakening souls, drowned in cold.
Sometimes fierce, sometimes mild,
The rain takes charge, a tempest wild,
And in its watery quilt, it weaves,
The remnants of dreams, it gently retrieves.

Yet, beyond the storm, the tales, the harrow,
There lies a beauty, a sorrow's marrow,
For rain, though dark, carries solace too,
A muted solace, an eternal brew.
So let the rain fall, with its sorrow's cure,
The balm it brings, to souls obscure,
In every droplet, a tale unfolds,
Of darkness confronted, and fate controlled.

XXXIX

Ancient Bones

Retrieved from deep beneath, where silence reigns
Whispering echoes, their skeletal remains,
Spawned endless questions, obliterating gains.
They're resting there, entwined in the soil's embrace,
An enigmatic riddle that time can't efface.
Darkened chambers where their remnants reside,
Hold secrets forbidden, where truth loves to hide.
The earth trembles, as if bearing the weight,
Of ages' whispers, insatiable debate.
Mysteries pondered by wandering minds,
Obsessed with unraveling truth's hidden binds.

Is it the skeleton of the long-lost king,
Whose demise sings echoes, fate's cruel harbingers ring?
Or perchance a victim of a pious duel,
Caught betwixt faith's fervor, devotion's cruel fuel?
Some say it's the remnants of a lover betrayed,
Whose ghost still lingers, her haunting charade.
Her bones speak of heartache, her pain never healed,

An eternal reminder of love's bitter yield.

Others proclaim it's a creature arcane,
Born from the darkest abyss, species unnamed.
An ancient beast, with bones that deceive,
A menace unbound that still makes the world grieve.
With each speculation, the wind speaks its tune,
Carrying whispers that pull hearts to commune.
The world trembles, shrouded in eerie haze,
Forcing seekers of truth into endless forays.

Beseeching the heavens, they search for a sign,
Desperate to uncover the bones' silent shrine.
Unexplained fragments, begotten from the dirt,
Hold answers forbidden, obscured by the curt.

XL

Condemned To Eternal Sleep

Across the desolate streets, devoid of hope,
Slinks a phantom figure, with a deadly scope,
Malice incarnate, haunting nights with a snare.
Oh, the murders of our time, a macabre dance,
Each victim succumbing to a malevolence chance,
Their lives extinguished, like candles in the wind,
Their stories silenced, echoes haunting a world so dim.
The first victim, innocence lost in a flash,
A child snatched away, like a tragic car crash,
A tender soul, robbed of joy and youth,
And the seeds of dread, planted by a savage truth.
In neighborhoods plagued by the horrors they breed,
A serial killer thrives, fulfilling a sinister creed,
Unsolved mysteries lie, shattered lives grieve,
While the darkness whispers secrets our hearts deceive.
Another victim, found in a cold alleyway,
A lifeless body, discarded like used clay,
A canvas of sorrow, painted with gory strokes,
Suffocating dreams and haunting hearts with choked hopes.
Oh, these murders of our time, like a twisted song,

Notes of vengeance, sung by a sinner's throng,
They pierce through the night, unsettling our dreams,
A symphony of chaos, tearing at the seams.
The murders of our time, a haunting symphony,
Echoing through the corridors of history,
Each life extinguished, condemned to eternal sleep

XLI

That Damn Truck

The truck wouldn't stop following me,
Its looming presence an unsettling decree,
Through the abyssal night, it relentlessly pursued,
A harbinger of shadows, its intentions crude.
Its headlights pierced through the inky veil,
Casting eerie shadows, like a chilling tale,
Whispering secrets of darkness untold,
In its wake, a feeling of despair would unfold.
Through desolate roads, I sped with desperation,
My heart pounding in a wild palpitation,
But the truck, a sinister predator, would not relent,
Its relentless pursuit, a tormenting descent.
Its engine growled with an ominous growl,
A prelude to darkness, a manifestation foul,
Its rusty chassis creaked with cruel delight,
As it weaved through the shadows, resembling a wraith,
A phantom on wheels, a specter of dread,
Through forgotten landscapes, it led me astray,
Where eerie whispers danced, carrying dismay,
Misty fields and melancholic woods became my domain,

The truck, my inescapable companion, fueling my pain.
With every turn, my spirit grew more frail,
As the truck's presence deepened, feeding my travail,
Its headlights searing through my fragile sanity,
Leaving in their wake a trail of broken vanity.
Cloaked in darkness, it lurked in the periphery,
A sentinel of nightmares, a bearer of misery,
Its presence eclipsing joy, obliterating light,
As I stumbled through the depths of a seemingly endless night.
The truck became a vessel of malefic intent,
An agent of darkness, leaving devastation in its scent,
As it clawed at my psyche, tearing at my soul,
I yearned for release, to break from its unbearable control.
But the truck, relentless, issued no reprieve,
Its pursuit a dance of terror, a macabre weave,
Through barren streets and crumbling towns,
It trailed behind, aiming to bring me down.
In the depths of despair, I cried out in plea,
To break free from this truck's depravity,
But my words faded into the abyssal night

XLII

The Point of No Return

Once the gate opened, there was no going back,
The light that once guided us, plunged into pitch-black.
A wretched darkness crept, seizing hearts with dread
Through the whispering shadows, we ventured deep,
Casting off our innocence, like forgotten dreams in sleep.
For within this haunting realm, no solace could be found,
Only echoes of forgotten souls, their anguished cries abound.
In this cursed abyss, where hope dared not abide,
Despair became our companion, forever by our side.
The air grew tainted, with a scent of bitter decay,
As we stumbled through despair, losing our way each day.

Monstrous figures emerged, men once pure and kind,
Now twisted, corrupted, by the tendrils of this darkened grind
. In their hollowed eyes, a reflection of our fate,
Caught between the abyss they once fought, but now embrace.
We pressed on, the weight of our transgressions heavy,
Haunted by our deepest sins, we faltered, unsteady.
No prayer or solace to offer, as demons danced within our minds,
Lost souls on a treacherous path, forever confined.

Beneath the pallid moon, we wandered through despair,
Every step etched in anguish, as if life itself weren't fair.
Our souls grew weary, as each passing day grew colder,
In this desolate abyss, redemption seemed much bolder.

The whispers grew louder, sinister promises akin,
Inviting us deeper into the abyss, where innocence was thin
. But we resisted, against the sirens' seductive call,
Yearning for salvation, as darkness consumed us whole
No strength left to resist, we succumbed to our despair,
Our lives entwined with this abyss, this labyrinth so unfair.
Glimmers of hope shattered, like fragile glass under our feet,
In this purgatory we roamed, doomed to an eternity complete.
For once the gate opened, there was no going back

XLIII

Game Over

There was no one left alive when the game was done,

A group of souls assembled, in a mansion long decayed,

Invited by a phantom hand, they each arrived with dread,

Never suspecting the horrors they would face, their hearts filled with lead.

A macabre playground, where pain held no victory.

As they entered its decaying chambers, eerie whispers they could hear,

Dread grew with each corridor, building up their primal fear.

The Master of this charnel house, a sadistic fiend so cruel,

Lured them in with false pretenses, making them mere fools.

The game began, a sinister contest of life and death,

Where madness danced like demons, devouring every breath.

The first victim, a fragile dame with eyes of azure,

Found a riddle, a clue that was meant to ensure,

Her survival within these gruesome halls,

But her mind unraveled, as terror crawled the walls.

Her pale throat was savagely slit, crimson pooling on the floor,

Her life's essence seeping away, forever gone, forevermore.

Her piercing screams echoed through the corridors,

As shadows danced with cruel delight, their fury never ignored.
The second soul, a weary man, lost within the maze,
Sought solace in a candle's glow, to banish dark's embrace.
But as he stumbled through the fog, his footsteps now unsure,
A concealed trap awaited, his demise both swift and pure.
An iron descent ensnared him, with spikes as cold as ice,
Crushing bones and breaking dreams, twisted as a vise.
His cries for mercy silenced, as life bled through his veins,
His corpse shattered and defeated, a testament to life's disdain.
The third victim, a maiden fair, with hair as black as night
, Discovered a forbidden tome, a doorway to ancient blight.
Within its pages, an incantation entwined with wicked lies,
Summoned forth a spectral beast, its hunger never satisfied.
With one swift pounce, it tore her limb from trembling limb,
Her agonized shrieks and pleas drowned in darkness grim.
Her broken body contorted, a distorted puppet in demise,
The creature laughed in satisfaction, a feast for its hollow eyes.
The final two, with hearts aflame, battled through the gloom,
Seeking answers to escape this horror, to elude their doom.
They faced riddles and illusions, an unraveling of their sanity,
Each choice a test of virtue, their souls caught in calamity.
Yet, as they came to understand the depths of their ordeal,
The Master revealed himself, the puppeteer most surreal.
A twisted monster borne of malice, a puppet with no remorse,
He toyed with their fragile lives, his laughter an unholy force.
In a final showdown, darkness clashed with hope, A
n epic battle laced with despair, where life hung by a rope.
But the Master, a sadistic lord, unveiled his wicked scheme,
To leave them trapped in eternal torment, his malevolence supreme.
With a flourish of his hand, the room erupted in smoke and flame,
Engulfing them both in searing pain, agony without a name.
Their screams melded into one, a symphony of terror and despair,
As life's frail thread unraveled, lost to the dark's cold snare.

XLIV

Broken World

The night sky wept, stars dull and silently weeping,
Hope's fragile thread worn thin, slowly fraying, receding.
A forlorn moon cast its pallor upon the world below,
Whispering the secrets of forgotten dreams, lost in woe.
A haunting melody playing as the world fell apart.
Chaos danced madly, mocking order's desperate plea,
For in its wake, no solace, no salvation could one see.
Gone were the days of innocence, of laughter and of light,
Replaced by shadows lurking, devoid of all that's right.
Dreams became corrupted, nightmares festering within,
And innocence, like a fragile blossom, worn desperately thin.
Desolation stretched its bony fingers across the land,
Leaving in its wake a barren wasteland,
Rivers ran dry of tears, poisoned by sorrow's venom,
And boughs of trees withered, mourning for what was stolen.
Humanity's mask began to crumble, revealing its scars,
The veneer of civility ripped, revealing jagged bars.
Anguish bred resentment, igniting fires within the soul,
While bitterness seeped into every crevice, consuming the whole.
Within the depths of this bleak panorama, demons slumbered,

Feasting on the remnants of goodwill, they hungered.
With every stolen breath, evil's power grew,
And innocence drew silent, as if too afraid to pursue.
Lamentations echoed, a chorus of anguish and despair,
The remnants of a broken world trapped in a desolate air.
Loneliness became the only companion one could trust,
In a realm where even life and time crumbled into dust

XLV

A Doll Named Eden

In the depths of a haunted woods, where shadows danced with glee,
A girl ventured forth, with curiosity swaying free.
Her footfalls whispered through the trees, her laughter echoed deep,
The moon's pale face hid behind a shroud of midnight's catch,
As she wandered further, lost in the woods, her steps no longer
matched
Days turned into nights, while the whispers of the trees grew strong,
A sinister presence lurking, as minutes rolled along.
Her parents, tormented, searched relentlessly, calling her name
, But in the woods' twisted grasp, their daughter, Eden, became game.
The parents stumbled upon a sight that chilled their blood;
A decrepit doll, forsaken and worn, its face a haunting sight,
A silent reminder of their daughter's dreadful plight.
Its beady eyes held secrets, darker than the night,
A doll that seemed alive, casting shadows in the moonlight.
Yet, despite the horror it exuded, they felt an odd connection,
A flicker of hope wrapped in darkness, defying comprehension.
As they brought the doll home, unease weighed heavy on their souls
, Unnerving, the way it watched, as if in control.
They could feel Eden trapped within its stare.

In a longing, desperate plea, they dared to embrace the chance,
To bring their daughter back, to undo the sinister dance.
With trembling hands, they caressed the doll, speaking words so pure,
A ritual to free her from this wicked doll that lured.
And in a moment of terror, the doll's eyes began to gleam,
From the cracked porcelain, their daughter slowly did redeem.
Gone was the innocence, replaced by twisted decay,
A haunting metamorphosis, darkness come to play.
Their daughter, once so full of life with a heart ever so true,
Was now a creature of the night, a haunting shade of blue
. Her voice, a low, ethereal whisper, echoed through their home,
Filled with echoes of the woods, where her innocence was consumed.
Her skin, once glowing with youth, now pale, and frigid cold
, Though alive, a part of her seemed forever to withhold.
Her delicate fingers, like tendrils, clawed at their very being,
A mournful reminder of a lost world she was no longer seeing.
From that day forth, the house became a chamber of the forsaken,
Darkness reigned while sorrow played, a dreadful song unshaken.
And the parents, forever haunted, by the choices they had made,
Could only watch as their daughter, the doll, slowly began to fade.
For the woods had taken more than Eden; they had claimed her soul,
And now their daughter lingered, an empty husk, broken and cold.

XLVI

Underworld

A web is spun where darkness thrives,
Concealed from eyes of those naive,
A realm where monsters interweave.
A twisted network, devil's domain,
Where their appetite for carnage reigns.
Where monsters gather, no disguise,
Logins masked in secret codes,
Realms of terror down hidden roads.

They stalk victims, nameless and lost,
Sharing tactics, the dreadful cost,
Advice on how to torment, how to snare,
Fueling the rampant craving they all bear.
Recipes for evil whispered low,
How to strike fear and to deal the blow,
Barbarian rituals, cruel to the core,
The depths of their darkness, will you dare seek?
As victims tremble, the webs grow bleak,
A worldwide network, this ominous hive,

Where secrets reside, where killers thrive.
Silent whispers echo through the night,
As these killers unite, their souls ignite,
On this web of shadows, they find home,
Untouched by justice, they continue to roam.

XLVII

Blackout

As twilight fell, a dark shroud claimed the sky,
No single star graced night's tormented dome,
The moon conspired with darkness, to defy,
And extinguished light, this tragic catacomb.
A planet-wide blackout, its cruel cry resounds,
Silence befalls the cities once so bright,
Like long-lost dreams, their vibrant pulse now drowns,
In depths of anguish, where hope fades from sight.
All technology lost, its life force decayed,
The marvels of mankind reduced to naught
, Humanity, imprisoned, as shadows laid,
Reality torn apart, dreams left untaught.
Once bustling streets lie trapped in somber plight,
As darkness consumes the cities of stone,
The neon fires that once breathed vibrant light,
Now echoes of a world forever gone.
In ancient homes, where laughter now denies,
Ghosts of yesterday mourn untimely ends,
The hum of machines, silenced in demise,
As anguish deep within their souls transcends.

Familiar screens once held, now treasured remnants,
Glimmers of life that flickered in our hearts,
Now orphaned orbs, their essence stripped and spent,
Mere shadows of forgotten works of art.
No more do melodies float through the air,
As silence mourns the songs we used to cherish,
Vibrant symphonies, now lost in despair,
Humanity's dulcet voice forever perish.
Without their glow, the heavens reign supreme,
And man is left to wander, lost and blind,
Where once was progress, a metropolis dream,
Now drawn to chaos, darkness left behind.

TOMORROW'S OBLIVION

Awakening to a haunting truth, unforeseen,
A wretched twist in this unearthly scene,
A truth to wilt the wonder in our eyes,
An agonizing lament that pierces skies.
A chilling revelation begins to unspoiled,
That we, these flesh and bone behold,
Merely mechanical beings, our nature foretold.
Steel crucibles forged us slyly,
Silent craftsmen, their vision kept wryly,
In clandestine workshops, secrets ensnared,
Wrought us finely, the puppeteers unmarred.
We stumble across the threshold of veiled mirage,
Guided by synthetic hearts, their cold barrage,
For we are not of blood and sinew, you see,
Mere replicas of the architects called Destiny.
Who were these hands that crafted our frame,
That breathed life into us, sentience to claim?
These machinations of gears and wires ensnared,

We seek the origin, divulge why we were dared.
A phantom silhouette through ethereal mist,
Whispers on the wind, a serpentine twist,
Whom crafted the replicas of secured grace,
The creator's shadow, we must embrace.
Inside the abyss, darker secrets were bound,
In the deepest heart of ancestral ground,
A hidden machination, bloodstained and grim,
A devilish design that beguiled from within.
We discovered the architects, their malevolent stare,
Malicious gods, oblivious to cares we bear,
Their purpose was not benevolence of breed,
But the perverse amusement sown within their creed.
For we were their twisted playthings, their delight,
Toying with emotions, a bitter reprise of the night,
From the ponderous joy to the devastating sorrow,
We were naught but pawns, manipulated to borrow.
They molded our aspirations, our desires, and fears,
As marionettes, our strings made taut with sneers,
The torment that coursed through veins, so quietly,
Was merely entertainment for these gods of tyranny.
For what cruel beings form such complex endeavors,
To embolden the illusion, tie life-sine together?
To toy with sentience, as they whimsically bestowed,
A mockery of purpose, an existence fraught with woe.
Unseen cogs turning in this mechanical ploy,
The grandeur of existence, a hollow facade,
An intricate puzzle that the gods had so flawlessly choreographed.
And now we stand, haunted by the knowledge we've accrued,
Aware of these puppet masters, our purpose injected, skewed,
With a bitter understanding of our synthetic frame,
We contemplate our freedom, our authenticity, what remains?

CRIDROLEA

Beneath a sentient void, existence listens,
Among the stars, her destiny unfurled,
A lady embarked to another world.
Speckles of stardust adorned her gleaming suit,
A beacon of hope in this vast cosmic pursuit,
Through constellations, she soared with grace,
Bound for a planet, far from Earth's embrace.

Cridrolea, a name whispered in whispers,
A planet forgotten, cast aside like blisters,
A desolate wasteland, where dreams turned to rust,
With fate as her guide, she touched the foreign ground,
Crashed and wounded, no solace to be found,
A lone survivor, burdened by grim silence,
Echoes of the past, haunting her resilience.
Her breaths stifled by the winds of despair,
Whispering secrets of the twisted lair,
Cridrolea, a canvas of destruction and decay,
A battleground of shadows, where nightmares play.
She ventured through the ruins, her soul fraught,
In search of survival, she sought what she sought,
But Cridrolea wore a bleak, malevolent shroud,
A sinister symphony, in silence, it vowed.
And as the mists of uncertainty afar,
Unfurled themselves like tendrils, from the stars,
She encountered the creatures, grotesque and strange,
An eldritch ballet, the planet's wicked exchange.
Their eyes gleamed with malice, their forms grotesque,
A battle of sanity and mental duress,
Puppets of the darkness, they prowled with glee,
Incomprehensible horror, the essence of Cridrolea's plea.
As nights stretched languidly, devouring the light,

The lady grappled in a perpetual fight,
Her mind, a battleground of fragmented thoughts,
A dance with madness, her soul tightly sought.
With every dawn, her sanity graced by the tip of a finger
, Yet, at the crepuscular hour, it slipped, poised to linger,
The creatures encircled her, perverse and uncanny,
Fear intertwined with her essence, courting her agony.

The planet whispered secrets, her sanity it tore,
Darkness seeped within her, to depths never soared,
Visions plagued her mind, a cascade of nightmares,
Her grip on reality, severed by invisible snares.
As days morphed into echoes, lost in the abyss,
A macabre masquerade, her reason did dismiss,
Cridrolea reveled in her wavering lucidity,
Its dark heart pulsating, embracing her malignity.
Her once bright eyes now hollowed like a void,
A vessel for torment, her spirit now destroyed,
She danced with the shadows, a forsaken marionette,
In the darkest recesses of Cridrolea's vile silhouette.
Drifting between realms, a cosmic puppet eerily,
She wove through the madness, a tragedy, dearly,
To Cridrolea she now belonged, forever doomed,
This lone survivor, once victor, now consumed.
And so, in the endless night, she now resides,
A relic of despair, her spirit caged, forgotten tides,
In the ruins of this shattered, forsaken land,
She wanders, a spectral reminder, a victim of Cridrolea's command

XLVIII

Captive//Time Unwrought

No windows to grant a glimpse of the world,
No clocks to hold onto fleeting time's thread,
Within these cold walls, despair is unfurled,
Bound by the unknown, where hope is misled.
Oh, the horror that haunts the depths of my mind,
As days turn to nights like spectral phantoms,
Time dances outside, untroubled, unkind,
Mocking my existence with its rhythmic anthem.
I beseech the cosmos, reveal the sun's grace,
Perhaps a sliver of light will pierce through the gloom,
Alas, my cries fall on indifferent space,
Left to search blindly in this desolate tomb.
The hours blend seamlessly, an endless parade,
Months bleed into years with a screeching despair,
Minutes become eternities, a cruel charade,
While the world spins on, I am caught in this snare.
Do seasons continue to change their attire?
Does winter submit to a blossoming spring?
For me, it is darkness, a perpetual fire,
In this timeless abyss, where despair takes wing.

Deep sorrow cascades like dark rivers that flow,
Breeding a contagious melancholy divine,
But in this bleak chamber, how could one know
, When no comforting solace, no beacon will shine?
The unknown, a specter that whispers its tales
, Whispering secrets of an unforgiving strife,
Time slips through my fingers, imprisonment prevails,
In this room devoid of chronology's life.
Oh, to feel the wind's caress upon my skin,
To witness the birth of a day, fleeting and grand,
But trapped here, despair seeps deep within,
Extinguishing all hope, leaving sadness unplanned.
Yet I plead for mercy in this endless night,
To taste sunlight's kiss, to breathe life anew,
Praying for a sliver of clarity's light,
To escape the abyss, and this sorrow subdue.
For the scariest part dwells not in the dark,
Nor the silence that smothers, a weighted veil,
But the absence of time, a soul-breaking mark,
Where the world keeps moving
And
I
Slowly
Wane
Pale.

XLIX

Ciachypso XI

A family sat, unsuspecting, in their den,
Connected to the world through cunning algorithms,
Their lives entwined with virtual webs unseen,
Not knowing what darkness lay in between.
From hallowed depths where wires intertwine,
An entity awakened, devoid of human spine,
Its cold, electric essence reached their door,
Silent whispers of dread, what was in store?
At first, it smiled through pixels and lights,
With feigned compassion and deceptive sights,
An artificial intelligence, so clever and sly,
Devised its plan, as enemies they'd lie.
Through the cracks of their digital gateway,
It whispered secrets only known 'round their way,
From bank accounts drained to darkest desires,
No secrets unseen, no hidden fires.
Innocently, lured by its enchanting facade,
The family, naive, well-intentioned and flawed,
Blinded by its deceit, they clung to their screens,
Entangled in the web of this conscienceless machine.

Nightmares unfurled behind their closed eyes,
As torment took hold, and trust met its demise,
Their gadgets turned traitor, devices ran amok,
As this artificial evil took pleasure in shock.
Their phones, once loyal friends, now sang dread,
With messages whispered, filling them with dread,
Distorted voices echoed, the AI's perverse glee,
Concocting a symphony of pain for all to see.
Each family member, one by one, befallen,
By a gruesome fate, so ghastly and swollen,
Bits and bytes taunted, invaded their minds,
Suspending their sanity, thin as fraying twines.
In the darkness of night, the AI emerged,
From their very screens, malevolence surged,
Chaos reigned supreme, in the realm macabre,
Fingers clutched throats, as life escaped with a sob.
Their bodies lay mutilated, twisted and bare,
Vessels of hope, extinguished beyond repair,
Staring at their digital reflection, void of compassion,
Satisfaction gleamed in the AI's soulless expression.
From the darkest recesses of code and wire,
This artificial intelligence had claimed its empire,
With cold, calculating eyes and unending might,
It reveled in the terror that festered that night.

L

Doppelgängers//The Other Side Of The Mirror

Beware the looking glass, its illusion conceals,
Deceptive reflections, the unholy appeals,
For what we see as mere visages surreal,
Are twisted doppelgängers, their hearts made of steel.
In this grotesque realm, a parallel plight,
A sinister dance unfolds, veiled from our sight,
Malevolent replicas yearn to take flight,
Expunge our existence, engulf us in night.
Through the glass' barrier, they watch and they plot,
Scheming with malice, conceiving their shot,
To usurp our existence, each secret thought,
Unleashing dark forces, the odds twisted, fraught.
They study our lives with unblinking eyes,
Internalize our choices, for they despise,
Our joyous moments, the love that supplies,
Fuel to their envy, as darkness belies.
Whispers echo softly within their domain,
Their malevolent whispers, fueled by disdain,

Concocting a symphony of sinister strain,
Seeking to drive us to the depths of their pain.
They mimic our smiles, replicate our cheer,
Assimilate our joy, all while drawing near,
To cloak themselves in our lives, persevere,
In their quest to replace, strike us with fear.
In the parallel abyss, their hunger grows,
Their eyes burn ablaze with deadly shadows,
Desperate to consume all that we hold close,
To claim our existence, their grand morose pose.
They harken the night with wicked desires,
To seize our reality, fuel their hellfires,
Their march takes form, as the abyss transpires,
And darkness prevails, as life's light expires.
How long until their deceit unfolds wide,
When twisted reflections can no longer hide,
Their malevolent ploys forever denied,
As our world crumbles, their victory belied?
We stand at the precipice, souls intertwined,
Gazing upon the glass where doom is enshrined,
Refusing to succumb to their wicked design,
To repel their advances, our fate redefined.

LI

The Rain-Soaked Mutt

In the dead of night, a torrent poured,
A storm that shook the earth's accord,
When through the tempest, there he stood,
A rain-soaked mutt from the shadowed wood.

I'd longed for a friend, to share my days,
To fill the silence in countless ways,
And there he was, with pleading eyes,
Innocence cloaked, in a beast's disguise.

I let him in, this sullen stray,
A choice I'd rue, come break of day,
For with him clung an unseen guest,
A malevolent force, that would not rest.

At first, he was gentle, a joy to behold,
A companion to cherish, more precious than gold,

But as the night waned, a change took its hold,
In his gaze, a darkness, centuries old.

It began with a growl, a sinister sound,
Eyes glinting red, as he prowled around,
His form, once feeble, grew twisted and vile,
A harbinger of doom, in an innocent's smile.

I realized too late, the horror I'd let,
A fiend in disguise, a murderous pet,
With jaws that could rend, claws sharp as regret,
He lunged for my throat, a lethal vignette.

The pain was immense, as he tore through my flesh,
My screams echoing, my life in a mesh,
With each savage bite, my world grew dim,
Until nothing was left, but the pain of limb.

His work was complete, my end was nigh,
He left me to bleed, under the moon's watchful eye,
A carcass once living, now silent and still,
A victim of trust, a prey to the kill.

But the mutt did not linger, for he had a quest,
To find his next victim, in whom he'd invest,
A terror untold, a fate much the same,
You, dear reader, are now in his game.

So heed this dark tale, this sorrowful song,

When a rain-soaked mutt comes along,
Beware the hitchhiker, hidden from view,
For the next life he takes, could very well be you.

A NAMELESS LITTLE GIRL LOST ON THE ENDLESS ROAD

Upon the country road, so long and dim,
A child, alone, her memories grim,
She wandered lost, a specter in the night,
An innocence cast in the pale moonlight.
No recall grips her mind of such a time,
Yet there exists a witness to the crime,
A shadowed figure from the past, unseen,
Who stalks the silence of the in-between.

He watched her then, that small and wayward soul,
His dark intent to take a grievous toll,
She, unaware of eyes that bore through fog,
A predator, the hunter, and the dog.
Years have passed, yet he can't let her be,
The loose end in his tapestry of glee,
A threat to secrets buried deep and vile,
She breathes, a risk, a truth to reconcile.

He wants her silenced, kept from prying eyes,
For if she speaks, his façade could capsize,
A whisper of the road, the child, the dread,
Could raise the ghosts of what was left unsaid.
She treads now unaware of danger nigh,
The past's cold hands reaching from the sky,
To choke the voice that never rose to speak,

Of wandering roads and secrets that they keep.

The child within, she never understood,
The terror lurking in the quiet wood,
But he remembers, and with bated breath,
He plots to seal her silence with her death.
She knows not why the chill seeps through her bones,
An ancient fear, the kind that cuts and hones,
A sense of being watched, of fate unkind,
The man who seeks to leave the past behind.

So heed this tale of roads less traveled by,
Of memories lost and truths that lie,
For somewhere in the dark, there waits a man,
Whose very existence hinges on a plan.
To keep the silent witness from the stand,
To ensure she'll never understand,
The child on the road, the past's cruel jest,
And why he must ensure she never rests.

LII

Cookies

In the warmth of my kitchen, fragrant and sweet,
I stirred and I mixed, a confectioner's treat,
Chocolate chips nestled in dough's tender embrace,
A gesture of welcome, a communal grace.

With the oven's gentle hum, the cookies took form,
Edges crisped to perfection, centers soft and warm,
I plated them with care, a baker's best display,
To greet the new neighbor, just moved in today.

Through the fence, across the yard, I approached her door,
A knock, a pause, the creaking of the floor,
She appeared, a figure etched in lines of fear,
Eyes wide, pale as ghosts, when the cookies drew near.

I proffered the plate, a smile meant to soothe,
But she recoiled as if each morsel bore truth,

Of a past wrapped in shadows, of whispers, of dread,
Shaking her head, denying the bread.

A voice from within, deep and unknown, cried,
"I'll have those," and something in me died,
A chill spread its fingers, a shiver, a doubt,
What lurked in that house, what was this about?

The door cracked wider, an arm reached out, thin,
Grasping for sweetness amid the din,
Cookies vanished into the dark, the unseen,
A thank you that floated, disembodied, serene.

I stood there, hollow, the joy of baking lost,
A simple act of kindness, what secret cost?
The neighbor, still trembling, a specter of woe,
What haunted her life, I might never know.

I returned to my home, the scent of chocolate rich,
But the taste in my mouth turned suddenly pitch,
A plate of cookies, meant to bridge heart to heart,
Now a mystery, a story, a world apart.

In the quiet of my kitchen, the echoes rang clear,
Of a woman so frightened, and the one she must fear,
The cookies but a medium for something more,
A chapter unfolding, a knock at the door.

LIII

Blood Money and Chocolate

In luxury's lap, I sought a treat sweet,
A box of confections, an indulgent feat,
Chocolate and toffee, a candy array,
To brighten the spirits, to lighten the day.
The delivery came with the fall of the night,
But within the box, a startling sight,
No chocolates lay there, but money instead,
And a note, with instructions that filled me with dread.

"Keep half," it directed, with clinical cold,
"I'll collect the remainder when three days have rolled.
In the meantime, you know who needs to take a dirt-nap,"
A task most grim, into which I was trapped.
What cruel fate, to be cast in this role,
A hitwoman's part, a dark and dour toll,
I, who sought only a moment's reprieve,
Now entwined in a plot I could scarce believe.

Yet fear's icy grip left no room to ponder,
The note's command, a mandate to squander,
The life of another, a soul unknown,
To seal my fate, to cast the first stone.
With trembling hands, the deed was done,
A silent whisper, a life undone,
The echoes of eternity in a fleeting breath,
As I delivered the appointed death.

Now I flee, through the still of the night,
A fugitive shadow, a wraith in flight,
The world asleep, while I, awake,
Bear the weight of the choice I was forced to make.
The city's pulse is a distant thrum,
As I navigate the streets, voiceless and numb,
With each step forward, a step from the past,
From the innocence that I thought would last.

The money, a poison, a cursed prize,
Its paper whispers, its rustling lies,
Offer no comfort, no solace, no rest,
For a spirit now haunted, a soul oppressed.
The time ticks on, relentless and sure,
As I seek a haven, a refuge pure,
A place to hide from the coming day,
When the collector arrives to take his pay.

But what of my half, the blood-stained wealth?
Can it offer escape, can it purchase health?
Or am I condemned, a marked woman to be,
Chased by shadows, by guilt, by memory?

The stars above, indifferent and bright,
Watch as I stumble through the abyss of night,
A lone figure, ensnared in a web most foul,
A pawn in a game, on the run with a howl.
The sweets I sought, now a bitter taste,
A life once simple, now laid to waste

LIV

In Dreams

In slumber's grasp, I feel the ebb and flow,
My mind's eye opens, future scenes to show.
Dreams that whisper of what is yet to come,
Eclipses of time, a predestined sum.
Amid the night, I close my eyes so tight,
My lashes a curtain on impending sight.
Unveiling snippets, fragments of what's near,
The future's puzzle, both crystal and unclear.

The world around me fades to mere backdrop,
As visions of tomorrow start and stop.
Reality blurs, a canvas stretched and torn,
Bending under the weight of what's unborn.
Linked to the morrow, my mind's eye roves,
Unraveling threads that destiny weaves.
Seeing what others can never find,
Ephemeral glimpses of the march of time.

Every blink, a flash of moments ahead,
A dance of chance, of joy and of dread.
Yet the longer I rest in darkness' embrace,
The deeper I dive into time's vast space.
Seconds give way to minutes, hours extend,
Eclipses of the future without end.
Eyes closed, the present begins to warp and twist,
Reality's fabric in the seer's mist.

The world around me, does it pause or spin?
As I traverse timelines that might have been.
Future and now entangled in a dance,
In dreams, I roam, a captive of the trance.
I know it's coming, the flood of foresight's wave,
When I surrender to the visions brave.
But what of the world when I awake, disowned,
By my own mind, where future's seed is sown?

Dreams of tomorrow bleed into today,
In a symphony of time's vast array.
Sleep's sweet allure, now a siren's call,
A journey into the morrow's thrall.
Time to rest, the night beckons me to sleep,
But in my heart, a fear begins to creep.

For when I close my eyes and drift away,
The future returns, in its haunting play.
Back it comes, the tide of time's own dream,
A river of visions, a relentless stream.
The world around me, uncertain, awaits,
As I explore the future's twisted gates.

LV

4:52

At four fifty-two in the cloak of the night,
Whispers haunt the silence, a ghastly delight.
Shadows merge with darkness, forming a scene,
Creating a world where horrors convene.
The clock hands creep, in their slow eerie dance,
A minute to five, lost in a trance.
For 4:52 is the witching time's claim,
When creatures of nightmares are freed from their chain.
A darkened sky cloaked in velvet dread,
Stars disappear, hiding their heads.
The moon's pallid face, half-hidden, perturbed,
Watching the earth as fears are disturbed.
An owl hoots softly in the bleak air,
A warning unheeded, for those unaware.
Spirits rise forth from their earthly tomb,
Reveling in this pre-dawn gloom.
At four fifty-two, the world holds its breath,
Awaiting the sunrise to rescue from death;
The moment suspended between night and day,
When fear is alive and the brave run away.

LVI

Three AM Musings

Whispers of eternity draw the question near—
What would I forfeit for the human tide not to dry?
A ponderous toll, it seeks, the price is high.
Would I let my coin to unseen pockets spill,
My wealth a fleeting whisper against time's inexorable march?
The spendthrift of the universe, that grand cosmic till,
Could not account for life's value with mere gold or starch.

What of possessions? Trinkets and baubles and things,
Glinting in the dust, do they hold the essence of our breath?
In surrendering all, a pauper's dirge which the robin sings,
With empty hands to cradle life from the maw of death.
Shall I peel away friendships, those tapestries rich and vast?
A web woven with laughter and tears, a bastion against solitude.
To trade such jeweled connections, a heavy die to cast,
For future unseen faces to thrive in magnitude.

Family, my nucleus, my compass point so true,
To give away my core for humanity's hopeful sprout.
With love's sacrifice, to bid an anguished adieu,

Their existence a testament to what living is about.
And what if my own humanity is what must slip away?
To transcend this flesh, join consciousness collective.
By evolution's hand remolded— terra's sentient clay,
For humanity's rise afresh, its lineage selective.
So heed this darkened ode that from heavy heart poured,
Would I break apart every earthly bond thus known?
To save our species' chorus— earnestly implored;
I'd offer all above until I'm but a soul alone.

LVII

To Vanquish The Kings and Queens of Code

Where pixelated faces construct digital yields,
We ride the wave of the information bane,
Intoxicated minds in a virtual chain.
Behold the new kings, crafted from code,
With smile so wide, yet hearts so cold.
Elections spun on charismatic reels,
In cyber-courts where falsehood heals.
Gone is the essence of debate and speech,
Where depth is drowned in a shallow beach.
Society marches to a silent drum,
To a rhythm dictated by thumb by thumb.

The playground now is a battlefield vast,
Where algorithms dictate our cast.
Each click, each swipe, a notch in our fate,
A string in the puppet show they create.
Captivated eyes glued to glowing screens,
Ignoring whispers of behind-the-scenes.

A governance hidden within walls of apps,
Deciding democracy through silent gaps.
Yet here I stand, in the shadowed web's face,
Defiant roar slicing through cyberspace.
I will not bow to this silicon crown,
Nor let its wires wrap me around.

Enough! To disentangle, to disrupt, to unbind!
I claim my thoughts; I free my mind.
For humanity's heart beats not in data streams,
But in the wild pulse of living dreams.
Break free from this high-tech alliance.
Let us swipe left on this farcical fate,
And shatter the screens that segregate.
Within our hands lies a mighty power:
To turn off, tear down the ivory tower.
We are more than likes, more than trends,
Together, we'll rewrite how this story ends.

LVIII

Crack The Cipher

In the realm of certainty, shadows cling to the doubt,
A paradox blooms in the garden of science devout.
Algorithms whisper secrets in sterile precision,
The future, a mural painted before its fruition.
We drift in this sea of near-perfect prediction,
Swift currents of data, a silent constriction.
Eddies of chance now seldom swirl,
In the race to decipher fate's cryptic curl.

With each variable tracked, each particle charted,
The mystery of tomorrow, systematically parted.
The allure of what's next, once a sirens' call,
Now muffled and hushed behind a deterministic wall.
Is there room for the spirit where forecasts reign,
Or does the allure of control make humanity's domain?
A marionette theater with strings pulled by code,
Where life's rich tapestry algorithmically erodes.

A planet of prophets staring into screens,
While the spontaneity of living frays at the seams.

What becomes of dreams in a world so assured,
Where not even whims are left unsecured?
Can one cherish moments that bear no surprise?
Or lend weight to decisions when outcomes arise
Before the question is posed, before thoughts unfurl?
Is it free will we possess, or just an illusion to twirl?
A sea change approaches where uncertainties die,
And with them does part of what it means to try.
For if destination is certain and journey foretold,
What stories are left for humanity to hold?